Baby animals in raintorest habitats

Bobbie Kalman

Crabtree Publishing Company

www.crabtreebooks.com

Created by Bobbie Kalman

For Emma Filomena, with love
Did you know that your Grandfather
was my "big brother"?

Author and Editor-in-Chief
Bobbie Kalman

Editors
Kathy Middleton
Crystal Sikkens

Design
Bobbie Kalman
Katherine Berti
Samantha Crabtree
(cover and logo)

Photo research
Bobbie Kalman

Print and production coordinator
Katherine Berti

Prepress technician
Katherine Berti

Illustrations
Barbara Bedell: pages 6 (top), 24
Margaret Amy Salter: page 14

Photographs
Digital Vision: page 12 (background)
Dreamstime: page 19 (caterpillar)
iStockphoto: page 19 (pupa)
Photodisc: page 14
Shutterstock: front and back covers and
all other photographs

Library and Archives Canada Cataloguing in Publication

Kalman, Bobbie, 1947-
    Baby animals in rainforest habitats / Bobbie Kalman.

(The habitats of baby animals)
Includes index.
Issued also in electronic format.
ISBN 978-0-7787-7732-8 (bound).--ISBN 978-0-7787-7745-8 (pbk.)

    1. Rain forest animals--Infancy--Juvenile literature.
2. Rain forest ecology--Juvenile literature. I. Title.
II. Series: Kalman, Bobbie, 1947- . Habitats of baby animals

QL112.K343 2011   j591.3'909152   C2011-902551-5

Library of Congress Cataloging-in-Publication Data

Kalman, Bobbie.
 Baby animals in rainforest habitats / Bobbie Kalman.
    p. cm. -- (The habitats of baby animals)
 Includes index.
 ISBN 978-0-7787-7732-8 (reinforced library binding : alk. paper) --
 ISBN 978-0-7787-7745-8 (pbk. : alk. paper) -- ISBN 978-1-4271-9716-0
 (electronic pdf)
 1. Rain forest animals--Infancy--Juvenile literature. 2. Rain forest animals--
 Ecology--Juvenile literature. I. Title.
 QL112.K353 2012
 591.734--dc22

                                                                2011013880

Crabtree Publishing Company
www.crabtreebooks.com   1-800-387-7650

Printed in China/082011/TM20110511

Published in Canada
Crabtree Publishing
616 Welland Ave.
St. Catharines, Ontario
L2M 5V6

Published in the United States
Crabtree Publishing
PMB 59051
350 Fifth Avenue, 59th Floor
New York, New York 10118

Published in the United Kingdom
Crabtree Publishing
Maritime House
Basin Road North, Hove
BN41 1WR

Published in Australia
Crabtree Publishing
386 Mt. Alexander Rd.
Ascot Vale (Melbourne)
VIC 3032

What is in this book?

What is a habitat?

A **habitat** is a place in nature. Plants and animals live in habitats. They are **living things**. Living things grow, change, and make new living things, such as new plants or baby animals. These elephant mothers have given birth to **calves**, or baby elephants.

What is a rain forest?

A **forest** is a habitat with many trees. A **rain forest** is a forest that gets a lot of rain. Some rain forests are in areas that have four **seasons** (spring, summer, autumn, and winter). Other rain forests, called **tropical** rain forests, are in areas where the weather is hot all year (see pages 6–7). This book is about tropical rain forests. Some tropical rain forests get rain every day. Other tropical rain forests have both a **wet season** and a **dry season**. In the dry season, it might not rain for months.

The elephants on the opposite page are forest elephants. They live in Africa. They have come out of the rain forest to find water to drink.

Where on Earth?

Tropical rain forests can be found on every **continent** except Europe and Antarctica. A continent is a huge area of land on Earth. Tropical rain forests are near the **equator**. The equator is an imaginary line that divides Earth into two parts. The weather at the equator is always hot. Millions of **species**, or types, of plants and animals live in tropical rain forests.

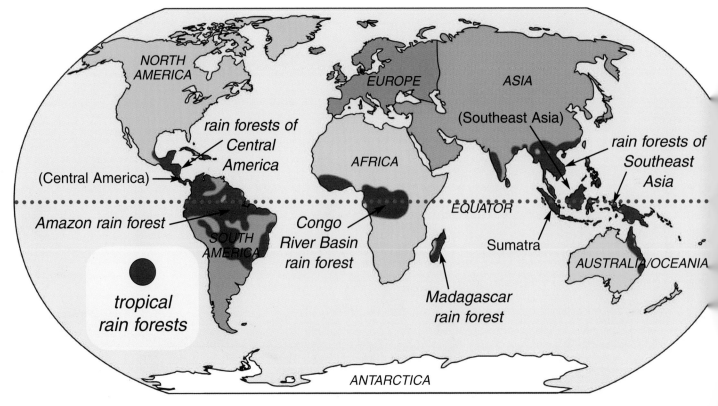

NORTH AMERICA

EUROPE

ASIA

(Southeast Asia)

rain forests of Central America

AFRICA

rain forests of Southeast Asia

(Central America)

Amazon rain forest

SOUTH AMERICA

Congo River Basin rain forest

EQUATOR

Sumatra

AUSTRALIA/OCEANIA

tropical rain forests

Madagascar rain forest

ANTARCTICA

South America

The Amazon rain forest stretches across nine countries in South America. It is the biggest rain forest in the world and has the most species of plants and animals. Rain forests are also found on the **coasts** and in other parts of South America. Coasts are areas of land near oceans. This baby Brazilian tapir lives in South American rain forests.

North America (Central America)

In the southern part of North America, there is a strip of land called Central America. Central America connects the continents of North America and South America. There are rain forests throughout the countries in this area. These baby capuchin monkeys live in a rain forest in Central America.

Africa

Africa's rain forests are found in the Congo River Basin on the west side of Africa and on the island of Madagascar. This young chimpanzee lives in the Congo rain forest.

Asia (Southeast Asia)

The rain forests in Southeast Asia are the oldest. They are found on many islands between Asia and Australia. This tiger cub lives in a rain forest on the island of Sumatra.

What do they need?

Habitats such as rain forests are made up of living and **non-living things**. Air, sunshine, water, rocks, and soil are non-living things. Living things need non-living things. They also need other living things, such as plants and animals. Living things find the things they need in their habitats.

Living things need water. This tiger cub has come to a river for a drink of water. It sees a fish and is trying to catch it. The cub is standing on a rock. Name all the living and non-living things in the pictures on these two pages.

Living things need food. The rain forest provides animals with many kinds of food (see pages 22–23). This mother dusky leaf monkey shows her baby which leaves are good to eat. Are leaves living or non-living things?

Rainforest babies

baby orangutan (Asia)

These are just a few of the baby animals that live in tropical rain forests around the world. Under each animal is the continent where it lives. Find the continents and rain forests on pages 6 and 7.

baby dusky leaf monkey (Asia)

baby ringtailed lemur (Madagascar, Africa)

forest elephant calf (Africa)

All the animals on this page can be found in rain forests in both South America and Central America.

baby squirrel monkey

baby sloth

baby caiman

baby macaw

jaguar cub

baby giant anteater

11

Layers of the forest

Many trees grow in rain forests. Different animals live in the different **layers** of the forest. The layers are called **emergent**, **canopy**, **understory**, and **forest floor**. The emergent layer is at the top of the tallest trees. Many birds, bats, and monkeys live in or visit these giant trees. The next layer down is the canopy. Sloths, birds, and tree frogs live in the upper parts of these trees.

This spider monkey spends much of its time in the emergent trees of the rain forest.

This young sloth lives in the canopy layer of the forest.

This baby margay lives in the understory of the rain forest.

The next layer down is the understory. Shaded by the taller trees, it is a cool, dark place where small trees and bushes grow. Many plants in this layer have large leaves to help catch sunlight. Margays, jaguars, and tree frogs live there. The forest floor layer is the ground, where insects, as well as giant anteaters, live.

young giant anteater

leafcutter ant

Mammal mothers

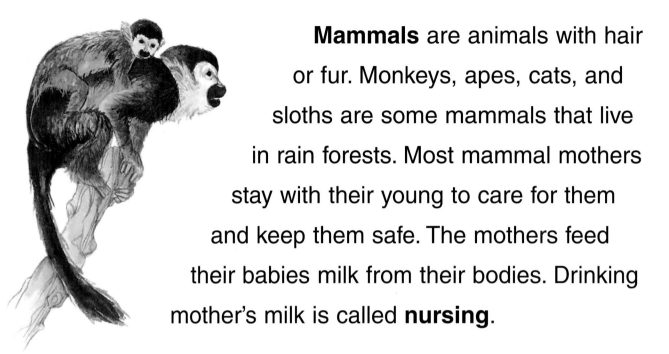

Mammals are animals with hair or fur. Monkeys, apes, cats, and sloths are some mammals that live in rain forests. Most mammal mothers stay with their young to care for them and keep them safe. The mothers feed their babies milk from their bodies. Drinking mother's milk is called **nursing**.

These tiger cubs are nursing. For about two months, milk is the only food they eat. They then start hunting small animals such as mice.

This mother and baby sloth are hanging from a branch.

This golden lion tamarin mother carries her baby on her back. Golden lion tamarins are monkeys.

This orangutan mother teaches her baby how to climb and swing from tree to tree. Orangutans are not monkeys. They are apes. Monkeys have tails, but apes do not.

Rainforest birds

Birds have wings and feathers, and they **hatch** from eggs. Many kinds of birds live in rain forests. They live in the different layers. Most parrots live their whole lives in the canopy and understory. Some fly up to the emergent layer to find food. They eat fruit, berries, and seeds. They also eat **nectar** and **pollen**, which is food found in flowers.

To hatch is to break out of an egg.

Baby parrots and other birds hatch from eggs.

These birds are Amazon parrots. Which is the baby and which is the mother?

Macaws are big colorful parrots. The macaw on the left is a baby. The middle one is a young macaw, and the bird with the long tail is an **adult**. An adult is fully grown. Macaws spend most of their time in the canopy and understory of the rain forest.

The bird on the left is a baby toucan, and the one on the right is an adult. Toucans have very large beaks. They use their beaks to reach fruit on the tips of branches. They also use them to dig holes in trees to make nests for their babies.

What is a life cycle?

Tree frogs live in rainforest trees. They start their lives inside eggs. They then become **tadpoles**, **froglets**, and adult frogs. The set of changes that animals go through is called a **life cycle**. Going through big changes in a life cycle is called **metamorphosis**. Frogs go through metamorphosis.

Baby tree frogs grow inside the eggs.

Adult tree frogs can make babies. This mother frog has laid eggs on a leaf above a pond.

The tadpoles grow legs and become froglets. As adults, they lose their tails.

Tadpoles with tails hatch from the eggs and drop into the pond.

underside

topside

A butterfly's life cycle

The blue morpho butterfly lives in the rain forest. Its huge wings are blue on the topside and brown with spots on the underside. The blue morpho's life cycle also includes metamorphosis. Each butterfly starts as an egg, becomes a **caterpillar**, then a **pupa**, and finally, a butterfly.

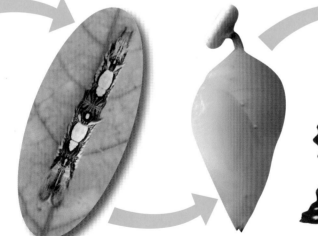

The blue morpho butterfly lays eggs on a leaf.

A caterpillar hatches from each egg.

The caterpillar hangs upside down and becomes a pupa.

An adult butterfly **emerges***, or comes out, of the pupa case and flies away.*

Water babies

It rains a lot in rain forests, so animals can usually find water in rivers, ponds, and **wetlands**. Wetlands are lands that are covered with water for part or all of the year. Fish, turtles, snakes, frogs, and birds are some animals that live in or near water in rain forests. River dolphins and caimans live in the waters of South American rain forests. Many other animals come to drink water at the rivers.

*Most dolphins live in oceans, which contain **salt water**, but the Amazon river dolphin lives in **fresh water**. Fresh water does not contain a lot of salt the way ocean water does. River dolphins eat fish, turtles, and crabs. This baby river dolphin has a long beak with over 100 teeth. How many teeth can you count?*

Caimans are small crocodiles. They live in rivers, lakes, and wetland areas of rain forests. This baby caiman is eating some insects. Later, it will eat fish, snakes, and mammals as big as tapirs and deer.

This mother capybara has brought her babies to a river for a drink of water. Capybaras are the world's biggest **rodents**. Rodents have four front teeth that never stop growing. They chew and chew to keep their teeth short.

A rainforest food chain

Living things need **energy**. Energy is the power to breathe, move, grow, and find food. All energy comes from the sun. Plants use the energy in sunlight to make food from air and water. Using sunlight to make food is called **photosynthesis**. Animals cannot make their own food. They must eat other living things to get energy. When one living thing eats another, there is a **food chain**.

What do animals eat?

Herbivores are animals that eat mainly plants.

Carnivores are animals that eat other animals.

Omnivores eat both plants and other animals.

The Amazon parrot is a herbivore.

This tree frog is a carnivore.

A squirrel monkey is an omnivore.